Five Reasons Why Your Organization Fails (Or Will Fail) to Reach its Stated Goals

Chetan Walia

ISBN-13:978-1507576816

ISBN-10:1507576811

Thank you Heena. Without your love and perseverance, I wouldn't have written this.

Contents

Preface

Not so long ago, I was attending a gathering of CEOs in Bangkok. The topic of the retreat was 'The Role of the CEO in the Modern World'. This topic was discussed and deliberated upon by prominent speakers and in several group discussions.

As far as I was concerned, the conference was a disaster. There was one problem. The problem was that there was no one to challenge the views of the participants. Thus, it became a self-validating exercise. Each delegate added what he or she was doing to the list of what every CEO should do.

I left that retreat midway with the conclusion that very few CEOs actually know what the role of a CEO should be.

Then I began my research. I intended to write a book on the role of the CEO. My team began interviewing CEOs, chairmen of companies, leaders in different fields, academicians, etc. We interviewed over 70 CEOs from different countries and companies, large and small.

We asked these leaders why their organizations behaved the way they did. We asked about their successes, their failures and their cultures. Interestingly, the interviews opened our eyes to the fact that the majority of the organizations around us are failing to reach their goals.

As I went through all the transcripts and data, I got a few insights into why organizations were failing to achieve their goals. This led me to expand the scope of my intended book from the role of the CEO to the larger question of why organizations fail to reach their goals.

On the basis of our conclusions, my company experimentally implemented the suggestions I have made in these pages. We worked on these with our clients, confirmed our conclusions, dropped those ideas the merit of which was not proved in practice, and finally, began to write a concise report on the findings.

The following findings are not mere reasons. They are root causes for failures. The entire research and thereafter this text has been written to help organizations identify root causes for their lack of expected successes.

I have intentionally kept this very brief and to the point to quickly get the message across to you and then get you to do the most important thing – act.

Here are the reasons why your organization might fail.

1

You Have the wrong map. Worse, you Believe it is the right One

Imagine for a moment that you are on your way to Shanghai. You do not read or speak Chinese, so the local people or the road signs would be of no use to you. You are, therefore, relying on your map.

For some strange reason, you have landed up in Beijing instead of Shanghai. You are trying to follow your map. You are doing your best. You are working very hard, almost nonstop, to make sense of what is happening. It gets you nowhere. You feel irritated, frustrated and stressed out.

What do you do? You do what an organization does. You call in an expert or your trusted adviser, who is sitting in the corner office on the sixtieth floor of a fancy, Big-four consultant's building in New York. Great, isn't it, to have such resources at your disposal?

Your expert consultant tells you, "Oh, no worries. My associate will just send you a report on best practices for a visitor in Shanghai. You will be out of trouble in a minute."

Within seconds, you are reading the best practices on your Smartphone. Now you are not only lost, but are also following the best practices meant for Shanghai, though you are in Beijing. Really, what are your chances?

By the end of the day, you are tearing your hair out and wondering what to do next. You scroll down your phone book, looking for the people you could call. You find a number. The number of your coach – the trusted, 'certified' adviser. Wow, he should be able to help!

So you give him a call and you feel better by the end of the conversation. He has brightened up your outlook, worked on your mindset and infused your attitude with positivity.

The next morning, not only are you lost in Beijing with a map and the best practices relevant to Shanghai, but you are also feeling good about it. Wow.

To me, that feeling sums up the colossal idiocy of a modern-day organization. The one which functions with the help of best practices, consultants and coaches. The one which incessantly reviews the implementation of ideas generated by these practices and consultants. The one which feels good and proud. The one which remains lost even after doing everything that everyone has told it to do.

The one which has a *wrong map*.

What needs to be changed is the map

Before you attempt to change behaviors and attitudes, what needs to be changed is the map. Before you try out your schemes, plots and best practices, what needs to be changed is the map. All in all, what needs to be changed is your map and your paradigm.

If you are in Beijing but following the map of Shanghai, it is pretty obvious that you will be lost no matter what you do, unless you change the map.

It is amazing that the obvious is not so obvious to an organization. Why not? It is not that they are dumb. There are reasons why they do not confront the problem of a wrong map.

(a) They do not know that it is wrong.

(b) Even when they know that it is wrong, the challengers have no solution, so they keep quiet about it.

(c) The map they are following currently works, at least to the extent that they survive.

Before you attempt to change behaviors and attitudes, what needs to be changed is the map.

In my eyes, the last reason is the most dangerous of all. The existing attitudes, strategy, best practices, thinking and behavior, and the coaches and consultants do produce some results. These results might not completely match the organization's potential, but in most cases, they still signify growth. So, an organization logically assumes that if things are working to some extent, they will go even better if they are done better or if certain issues related to implementation and execution are fixed.

That 'better' does not come. The truth is that you can go only so far with a wrong map. Eventually, the growth rate stagnates, and then starts declining. After this, the organization may discover the new map, though most do not. They either shut down, sell out, merge or just disappear.

As mentioned earlier, the first reason why organizations fail to reach their goals is that they have the wrong map. Let me elaborate further. What is this map? The map that almost all organizations around the world follow today is the map of accounting. In this map, human beings are considered expenses, though furniture is seen as assets. That is disgusting.

When you go by an accounting map, that is when your organization takes decisions based on accounting, what happens is as follows.

You set goals that are based on information received at your end. You then allocate budgets on the basis of the plans submitted by your departmental leaders. The plans they submit, both for the goals and budgets, are based on the performances (or deficits) of the previous year, as well as your expectations for the current year.

To assess the progress with respect to these goals and plans, you conduct review meetings, whether monthly, quarterly or biannual, depending on your system. What do you review at these meetings? Numbers.

And you discuss why the numbers are on or off the mark? And if these numbers are off the mark, you come up with an agenda of action items to correct these numbers before the next review meet. In the next review meeting, the process is repeated.

At some point during your review, you also discover that a team is demotivated, or that an individual lacks the appropriate skills of strategic thinking, or that a department needs inputs from some experts. So you commission some learning initiatives in accordance with your budget.

Doesn't this sound like an equivalent of being in Beijing with a map of Shanghai and calling in the experts to help you out?

There are retreats, training and coaching. But all your work leads to either marginal increases or marginal decreases. The year passes by quickly and you reach another goal-setting period; you have to draw up another budget sooner than you think.

Some heads will roll. Some new bright sparks will join the organization. In most cases, no one will be able to provide the breakthrough that the organization is hoping for.

At no point in the entire process of managing does it occur

to you that the map you are following is an incorrect one. The reasons for this are easy enough to understand. One is that the strategies are working to some extent. Another is that you think that this is the way everyone functions and is supposed to—the classic B-school syndrome.

This book does not intend to suggest that you abandon accounting principles. It aims to make the point that management through accounting does not help you achieve your potential. Again, the reason for this is simple, as described below.

Management by accounting measures efficiency.

You set goals. You set the key areas in which you want results or the key performance indicators (most of which are accounting in nature). You set these with respect to sales, marketing, production, logistics, human resources, finance, customer service and all your other departments. They are smart and they are measurable. They interlock nicely with your balanced scorecard, ready to be measured by the Bell Curve or by your grading system.

At the end of the year, you measure efficiency through percentages. Someone is at 80% and someone at 90%, or even 110%. Your company grows by a million or ten million, or by 5% or 10%, or whatever metrics you use. Whatever the growth or the lack of it, most boards observe that it is far below the organization's potential. In our research, there are very few organizations who manage to achieve their stated goals, year after year.

Measuring efficiency in this manner might, in fact, just mar the chances of making a breakthrough. That is because this type of assessment encourages people to create a culture of individualistic achievement, that is, departmental achievement. For example, the sales people are concerned with only the sales department, the production people with the manufacturing department, and so on. What is wrong with that? Everything.

Let me give you an example. I recently participated in a discussion at a 'sales meet' of one of the largest hardware manufacturing companies in the world. The discussion was on 'premium pricing' and market share. During the brainstorming, the team members could come up with ideas related only to their own domain, that is, policies, schemes for channel partners, marketing gimmicks and the like.

When I suggested that they evaluate a different value proposition for the customer that would make them more attractive than the competing companies, they argued that this was not really possible since they were a commodity market player.

I then suggested that a strategic value proposition could be created even within a commodity business for a channel partner through better logistics (availability), finance (making quicker payouts than the competitors) or the plant (quantity of the product), or even by offering marketing as a service (helping the channels increase their business).

I came up with specific solutions for them on how each department could create a USP for the channel partner. I got absolutely blank looks for a response. They had got the point and seen the logic. The sales team of one the largest manufacturing companies in the world could not figure out how to get the other departments to consider this suggestion. There was a logical reason for this. It was not the other departments' goal. The performance of the staff of the different departments was being measured by different criteria. It would not be a priority for them to cooperate. The sales department felt, 'We will lose if we rely on them.'

Efficiency isn't the goal of any business.

I can tell you what will happen in this company at the end of the year. The sales team will manage to contribute some face-saving marginal increase in growth. The other departments will manage their percentages according to their performance parameters. The organization will manage its marginal growth.

Collectively, they will not even realize that they have lost the chance to make a potential breakthrough, merely because they did what they were meant to—being efficient.

Following an accounting-based map that guides the members of your organization to be efficient takes away their ability to collaborate in order to produce a breakthrough. Sadly, a breakthrough does not take place in isolation. Moreover efficiency isn't even the goal of any business.

The performance of an organization depends on the interaction between many variable parameters, people and departments. To produce breakthroughs and extraordinary results in a sustainable manner, an organization must create a synergistic culture. The 'management by accounting' organization cannot do that.

The profit that an organization generates has to be a result of managing. The managing need not be a result of accounting. Your account book is an outcome of the means, not the means to an outcome.

To summarize, a 'management by accounting' organization gives rise to a culture in which performance is measured in terms of individualistic or departmental efficiency, and this essentially (whether acknowledged or not) makes for a number-driven rather than value-driven organization. For an organization to be able to provide value to the customer, collaboration between the many faces of the company is essential. However, the accounting principle, i.e. that of efficiency in setting goals and drawing up the budget, prevents this from happening.

The emphasis of this argument is not that one should not have budgets; it is that accounting and efficiency cannot be the key criteria for decision-making because this is self-defeating. It creates an individualistic culture that destroys the potential creation of value through collaboration.

The second reason why your organization may fail to achieve its goals is as follows.

2

Yours is not a value-driven company

A value-driven company means something other than providing value to a customer. In order to understand this, let us ask the question, 'Why does an organization exist?'

Any organization, (large or small), product or service exists to create and serve customers. That is its fundamental function. If an organization does not have a customer or does not create and serve enough customers who reward it with a fair remuneration, it will cease to exist. An organization existence, as well as growth, depend on the creation of more customers and its ability to derive more value from customers.

A very logical way to create more customers would obviously be to continuously create greater value for them than is created by their other options.

You may argue that you create value for the customers because you supply them with a great product or service. In today's world, that is insufficient and does not qualify you as a value-based player. It does not suffice because it is a threshold requirement. Customers buy a product or a service for a reason. They do not buy products or services because of all the requirements they may fulfill.

In today's highly informative and technologically advanced world, your product or even your service will not remain unique for long. Yes, your product or service may have a compelling advantage that cannot be copied. However, this does not mean that another competing product cannot satisfy the end need of the customer.

I provide consultation services to two of the Big Four consulting companies. I know all four quite well. All of them pride themselves on their business advisory services. All of them believe that their methodologies of research and their analyses are of unique value, enabling them to provide better advice to businesses or to their clients.

However, this is irrelevant from a customer's point of view. The customer is looking for an end result and I do not think that the customer really differentiates between the four on the basis of these parameters. The result is that none of these companies is able to stand out to any significant degree in the eyes of the customers. All of them thus face a constant 'price' pressure and under cut each other.

Even though you may have a differential product or service, it does not get converted into a product or service of unique value to the customer in any sustainable way. In today's world, the minimum expectation out of being in business is to bring value beyond the product or service. Thus, the way forward is to make your company a value-driven one, rather than continuing as a company that merely provides a valuable product or service.

Many of those who create good products fall into the trap of arrogantly believing that they are assured of customers since their product is outstanding. However, customers go to value-based, value-driven organizations.

Every search engine on the web can do what Google does; almost every mobile phone—even the cheap Chinese ones—can perform all the functions that an Apple performs; and every good online store will provide you with deals similar to those provided by Amazon, and some offer even better ones. Similarly, many smaller consulting firms provide you with solutions that are better than what the Big Four offer.

It is not just about a unique value in a product or service. This doesn't remain unique. This value is considered a threshold requirement. What will give you a breakthrough is a value-driven organization and not merely a valued product or service.

What is a value-driven organization? Let me go on to explain. It follows a value-driven map as against an accounting map. You must ask yourself, "What does my customer consider to be value?" The answer to this should be the minimum that your organization delivers. This 'minimum' is where all organizations will eventually be in the value chain.. Value-driven organizations start at the minimum and go on to drive value from there on.

I was providing consultancy services to a software company which has an outstanding proprietary product. However, it is not reaching its goals. So what is it doing? It is investing its time, money and resources in the creation of an even more outstanding product. The company is completely consumed by its love of its technology and its arrogant stance that its product is so good that the customer would be a fool to buy something else. In reality, the customer does not care what the companies think. This company possessing one of the most advanced technologies in the world had remained stuck because they failed in value creation for the customer in its other departments.

What will give you a breakthrough is a value-driven organization and not merely a valued product or service.

Most organizations are in the dark about the value they provide. As mentioned earlier, most are 'accounting map' organizations, in which it is largely the responsibility of the sales, marketing or customer service teams to source business, while the other teams have their own budgeted goals. This is where the organization falters because very soon, the sales people are attempting to sell products and services of obsolete value (which has already become a norm in the industry as it is being offered by others). The organization does not take cognizance of this and arrogantly keeps pointing out subtle and technical differences between its products/services and those of others—differences which, in reality, do not matter to the customer.

The solution, as I said earlier, is to create a value-driven organization. The rest will come almost automatically. An organization has several departments—sales, logistics, marketing, finance, information technology and so on. In a value-driven organization, each department should be able to answer this question: *What is the unique value that our department is creating and providing to the customer?* Do not confuse this with internal customers.

Whether it is in the department of human resources, information technology, finance or research and development, everyone in the organization needs to work in tandem and be externally focused on creating and providing value to what is the reason for a company's existence, i.e. the customer, else they may as well cease to exist.

Each department has to give the organization a unique strategic advantage. The collective effect of these advantages will create a value-driven organization, which will then be in a position to exploit multiple vehicles to generate a breakthrough.

Most organizations rely on a single vehicle, that is, a single

USP, to succeed. This is mindless because an organization can make use of so many other vehicles on which it is already incurring a fixed cost. Doesn't it make sense to do some rethinking so as to enable each of the vehicles to deliver value?

In the event that an organization fails to do utilize its multiple vehicles and relies on a single vehicle for the provision of value (for example, product or quality), it will very soon find itself in a survival mode, scrambling for existence or for marginal growth. This is because every company on earth has at least a single vehicle.

Most organizations rely on a single vehicle, that is, a single USP, to succeed. This is mindless.

To create a value-driven organization, it is imperative for the organization to be a collaborative one because in this way, each function will rely on the feedback and inputs of the others, helping to create value for the customer. The value generated by each department must be synergized for the customer to actually derive value from the purchase. It is thus essential that the central parameter of an organization should be synergy between its departments rather than individual efficiency.

As pointed out earlier, the accounting map creates an organization which is based on efficiency, in which people and departments are more worried about their 'part' than about the 'whole'. This happens because someone has to be held accountable. It is the departmental boss, rather than the team, who is made accountable. The boss, in turn, makes individuals accountable by setting his own key areas in which he wants results and to which he allocates budgets. The individual starts focusing on his 'part', leaving little room for synergy even within a department, to say nothing of synergy among all departments. This is the third reason for the failure of organizations.

3

Organizations create individual accountability and not team accountability

The guidelines that we follow for management and the processes and tools that we use are part of a mindset. A fixed mindset.

Management, at least at a 'profit for organization' level, is a relatively new practice. It has evolved over the last century. The pattern for how companies are managed has been set more or less by a few books, a few best practices and a few success stories. Every company adds a few twists to its own system, but the pattern is largely the same. Even the MBAs in universities all over the world are similar. Yes, there is a difference in terms of the quality of education and experience, but not so much in the framework of what the students learn.

When we consider the way we think about business or growth, therefore, we are convinced that 'this is the way'. Even the individuals working in an organization have similar goals and ambitions. All of them want to be managers or functional leaders or CEOs. They feel that this is what will earn them recognition and respect in society. For this reason, these positions of power are the most sought after goals.

In the individual's estimation, these designations make a 'hero' out of her, validate her choices in life and boost her self-worth. Everyone strives to be this hero. Managements are constantly looking for these heroes (or stars or champions), who they believe can propel the organization forward and help it to achieve its goals. The current system of management, with its fascination for heroism, fits in wonderfully well with our society as well. After all, hero worship or the phenomenon of being star struck is omnipresent, and has been so for hundreds of years.

So where is the problem? And why is there a problem if the system works? It can be argued that the system works because companies with this mindset are successful. Then again, the way you define success is also reflective of a mindset.

The success of the organization is not reflected in how much it will grow tomorrow. It is reflected in whether or not it will exist in the next generation and the next.

Your marginal successes or market growth or expansion are not successes. These are related to temporary market conditions. They are not sustainable. They are not long-term achievements. The proof of this is that if these systems and mindsets worked successfully, then companies would survive longer than they do. But they do not; they die.

Eighty-six per cent of the companies mentioned in the Fortune 500 list just fifty years ago do not exist any more. Only thirteen percent of businesses successfully progress onwards to the third generation of entrepreneurs. Eight out of ten companies that are backed by serious and experienced venture capitalists do not even see their third year of existence.

What does this tell you? The great historian, Arnold Toynbee, sums up the history of the world in four words: "Nothing fails like success."

An organization with the mindset of following an accounting map fixes individual accountability. Organizations do this consciously. Targets are allocated to individuals. Performance indicators are drawn up and people are assessed individually at the end of the year. This sets the stage for making the so-called high achievers heroes.

These heroes attain positions of authority. They have obviously learnt by now that success is an outcome of a good individual performance or good contributions, and over a period of time, this outlook becomes established.

However, as the organization goes down this road of success, there comes a point where it hits a roadblock. Either it stops growing fast enough, or it is unable to break some shackles. Yes, organizations may grow through acquisitions and new ventures at this stage, with their heroes perhaps bringing increase in numbers again. However, they will hit a roadblock.

There is a reason for this. The heroes either lose their motivation or hunger, or in some cases, genuinely do not possess the capability to think their way out of certain situations. At this point, one of the heroes becomes the target of the other heroes in the system. The blame game and mudslinging ensue.

The human resources department of the company manages the situation well. It conducts some training designed to help the people get along well with each other. Things probably get back on track for a while, but the problem recurs. Whether in three months, six months or a year, the problem comes back. And it is worse when it comes back.

Why does it come back? The answer is simple—you did not deal with it completely. You didn't address the root cause. The fact is that the success of the organization is not reflected in how much it will grow tomorrow. It does need to grow in order to exist, but its real success lies in whether or not it will exist in the next generation and the next. The seeds for this kind of survival are sown now and the germs for the failure to survive are also injected now.

In our companies, the individual is made accountable to his

bosses. The buck stops there. She is the boss, the decision-maker.

Our performance management systems (PMSs) play a big role here. They measure individual performance, point out weaknesses and fix accountability. PMSs act more like systems to detect weaknesses and penalize people.

"A group of donkeys led by a lion can defeat a group of lions led by a donkey."

In our performance reviews, the boss is equally responsible as her team for her team's output. When her team is not producing the desired results, what does She do? She does what most heroes in our films would do. She uses her majestic power to thrash the enemy. She wields her power and takes a few decisions. She wants to prevent mistakes because that is what her performance reviews have taught her. So She wants to be better informed and in control of most things, or wishes to direct them. Now no big decisions can be taken without her.

The team members conform with this dictate. Hero worshipping is convenient for them, except for the fact that they might not like this hero. They still abide by her decrees.The teams start speaking the boss's language—that is what the boss wants to hear. Never mind what the right thing to do may be; they do the acceptable thing, which is to conform to the directives of the boss.

Socrates said, "A group of donkeys led by a lion can defeat a group of lions led by a donkey." A system of individual accounting reduces our very talented lions to donkeys receiving instructions. These teams will no longer produce any breakthroughs because they do not even think. They have learnt and mastered the art of survival through conforming to a norm. The norm is the boss. The boss will reward them for conforming.

This boss will probably never produce a leader who is better than her. How can she, when she is the one who decides everything?A combination of such teams will ensure that the organization hits a roadblock. Once it does, the leadership will be more or less clueless because as far as it is concerned, it did everything right. Their performance ratings will serve as proof.

You can bring in consultants. You can bring in the Big Four. You can bring in the best professionals to educate you. It will not work. It will not work unless someone helps you change your map.

You know very well that the business is a team game. You

know very well that your teams need to be able to perform for you to do better. You know that your organization's output is a direct result of the output of your teams. You know that collaboration is the key to success in any interdependent environment, like an organization. Your documents on your values and visions probably have the words 'teams' and 'trust', or synonyms of these, splashed all over them.

Then why on earth do you make individuals accountable and not teams?

The teams need to be accountable.

Performance management systems need to measure the performance of teams. They should create a dedicated culture, and not a culture in which the team has to ask the boss what to do. What is the purpose of accountability? Why is the need for accountability? The basic purpose is to ensure that you do not fail. What will ensure success in an organizational scenario? Heroism or synergy? What is synergy? The best way I can define it is thus: The whole is greater than the sum of the parts.

Breakthroughs are produced by a culture of synergy, or a culture in which people collectively look for better solutions; in which people are free to interact, communicate and challenge; in which people are not thinking of what the leader wants to hear; and in which people are accountable to each other because they know they are assessed as a team. Only then will their energy be transformed into creative energy, and only then will the lions behave like lions and not like donkeys that are conforming.

But how do you create this culture? How does the leadership create such an organization? Where does one start? Well, you start with the leader, who can do this for you. The leader has to start exercising moral authority, and not formal authority. This brings us to the fourth reason why organizations fail to reach their goals.

4

Leaders lead by exercising formal authority, not moral authority.

We really need to have a clear idea of what leadership is. It is only then that we will be able to transform a successful organization into a breakthrough organization.Why is leadership relevant? Leadership defines an organization's culture. Consciously or unconsciously, the organization follows or adheres to the culture that emanates from the behavior of its leader. It may also go by the leader's perceived behavior.

A leader has a certain belief system. She has certain ideas about how things ought to be done and how the organization should proceed to achieve its goals. Her belief system is her culture. Generally, an organization will never rise beyond this belief system because the followers will very quickly adapt and adhere to this system.

Haven't you witnessed a situation in which someone in an organization is trying to question something and her bosses put her in her place by saying, "That's the way the boss wants it." End of argument! "Do as I say, not as I do." This does not work.

Your leadership sets the tone for your organization's culture and this culture, in turn, determines your achievements and non-achievements.

We may spend a lifetime trying to change the behavior and attitudes of the people in an organization in the hope of improving their performance. This has very short-term, or no, results at all. This is because what we need to change is the culture.

As discussed earlier, an organization is much more likely to succeed in an environment marked by synergy than one characterized by individual accountability. This is not mere behavioral change. *It is a cultural transformation.* It is the leadership that will set the tone for a cultural transformation because it is the leadership that has introduced the current culture in the first place.

If you find that people in your organization are unable to do things differently despite being told to do so repeatedly, it is not because they lack the ability; it is because they are unable to in the organization's dynamics of interdependence .

As outlined earlier, the same culture that helped an organization grow to a certain level might become a roadblock to further growth because you can only go that far with a wrong map.

All organizations focus on creating a high-performance environment and the creation of a performance-driven culture. In the process, they ignore the most common sense logic and the fundamentals. They start to follow an accounting map, coupled with the individualistic fault-finding PMS. They ignore performance.

What is performance in an organizational context?

Performance is interdependent—dependent on other people, functions and teams. You cannot climb Mt. Everest alone. You need a team to manage a thousand other activities. You do not need a team that will be competing to see who gets to the top first. You need a team that will make the mission successful, irrespective of who reaches the top first.

The team members will make the mission successful if they are encouraged to work together, if they are accountable to each other and if they are jointly accountable for the task, and not if just the head of the team is accountable. If people are held individually accountable, you will find that each one will feel that they have done well – the reason for the overall failure will always be external according to them. This gives rise to an environment that is counterproductive.

What role does the leader play in creating this culture? *The leader's role is to create a leader. Period.* Anything that a leader is to accomplish has to be done through creating leaders. If a leader has become the 'central authority' for her team, she has already failed, for everything depends on her. Her team, too, will fail because in no time, it will become convenient for them to let her decide everything. Thus, it is largely she who remains accountable. And this suits everyone in the team. You will find that the heads of such teams change frequently. The culture does not.

The leader has to create a culture which fosters an organization that is value-driven and profitable.

At the heart of the organization is its culture. The culture decides how the other parts of this body will move and communicate with each other.

The leader's role is to create leaders. Period.

Moral leadership entails the creation of leaders by the leader, such that the leader becomes almost irrelevant. In the case of formal leadership, the leader is accountable and so it is she who decides (rules).

A leader needs to become irrelevant. That is clearly the path to making the organization function successfully. It is only when she creates leaders that she will be able to create a culture in which people are committed through a feeling of psychological ownership. Psychological ownership will emerge because when the leader develops leaders, the latter will be able to perceive their own value through the experience of leading by themselves.

Greatness has four elements: to live, to learn, to love and to leave a legacy. Every human being aspires to these. Whether as a leader or an ordinary human being, one must ask oneself, "What is the legacy that I am leaving behind?" After everything is over, all that people will remember you for is the difference you made to them.

This re-emphasizes the point that leaders must create leaders. That is the way an organization grows. That is the way a society grows. That is the way a nation grows. That is the way the world grows. That is the way a leader herself grows.

When trying to develop a successful culture, there are three imperatives that a leader must keep in mind.

(a) The first imperative is to inspire trust.

An entire book could be devoted to this point alone and in fact, a book called *Speed of Trust* has already been written on the subject. However, for the purpose of this book, I would like to mention behaviors, characteristics or qualities without which a leader can never inspire trust.

The foundations of moral leadership are integrity, orientation to service and humility.

(i) Integrity

Integrity is one of those words that are thrown about by people in their value and mission posters. I have great doubts that they even understand it, let alone practice it.

In the simplest practical terms, integrity means doing what

you say and saying what you did. This is how people interpret integrity—through words and actions. Period. If you do something other than what you said or say something other than what you did, you do not have integrity. You will not have moral leadership. You will not be able to leave behind a lasting legacy. You will be forgotten.

In the simplest practical terms, integrity means doing what you say and saying what you did.

If we look back on history, the reason why there are only a few leaders whom we hold in high esteem is not that many of them lacked a large vision. Plenty had big dreams and plenty still do. The reason is that only a handful had a high level of integrity. Even fewer do today.

Leaders or organizations compromise on their integrity mostly for some short-term gains. They claim that they are committed to the value of integrity, but business or economic realities dictate another path. The bald truth about integrity is that either you have it or you do not. There is no such thing as partial integrity.

If you hope and need to inspire trust in your people and have been unable to do so, you will always find the root cause in integrity. For one to be perceived of and accepted as a leader (by moral authority) it is absolutely essential to have the highest level of integrity. In the absence of this quality, leaders lose the trust of the people and then resort to authoritative means—the beginning of a cultural collapse.

There is absolutely no way to inspire trust in followers in the absence of integrity. You will find a very simple of proof of this if you introspect on the way you vote when electing your leader.

(ii) Being service-oriented

Remember that you are essentially trying to create a value-driven organization. Thus, the leader needs to create a culture which helps to make the organization a value-driven or service-oriented one.A leader leads a group of people essentially to accomplish a mission or fulfill the vision or goals of an organization.

Leadership is not a title. It is a moral responsibility to get others to achieve more than they would have without the leader. Thus, the goal or the purpose of leadership is of prime importance. In other words, the leader must constantly serve the purpose of her leadership. The primary purpose of a leader is to develop other leaders who will achieve the goals and visions of the organization.

In the simplest, practical terms, orientation to service is doing the right thing versus the acceptable thing.

We are constantly faced with choices and decisions. In this, we have to choose between the right thing to do and the acceptable thing to do. Many leaders fall into the trap of doing the acceptable thing.

For example, in many situations, the acceptable thing to do might be to compromise integrity, keeping the short-term gains in mind. Is that the right thing to do?

In the simplest, practical terms, orientation to service is doing the right thing versus the acceptable thing.

The acceptable thing to do is to follow an old mindset and create structures of formal authority and individual accountability, on the basis of an accounting map. Is this the right thing to do in the interest of an organization and its customers?

The acceptable thing to do is to find reasons for the organization's current problems and blame others for these. And maybe, other than blaming other departments in your organization, blame the world economy, political leaders, etc. Is this the right thing to do? Does it help improve anything?

The acceptable thing to do is to have endless, fault-finding review meetings that last for hours. Does this really help you?

The acceptable thing to do is to hire consultants who are big shots and cost millions to solve your problems. Have they ever solved the problem you hired them for?

The acceptable thing to do is to emulate best practices from other organizations and implement them. Does it work? Did it even occur to you that these practices are best suited to a certain culture and not yours?

A leader must do the right thing, that is, the thing that serves his mission, organization, people and customers. In doing what is merely acceptable, she is abdicating responsibility and losing the people's trust.

(iii) Humility

In the simplest, practical terms, humility in the context of leaders is to become irrelevant by creating leaders.

We have a wrong notion of leadership. At their meetings, in the reviews they carry out and in their very personas, leaders, managers and executives endeavor to be seen as people who are in charge and in control. The purpose of leadership is not to be seen as a leader. It is to create teams that will lead people to accomplish the mission.

It is only when a leader possesses humility that She will be able to shift her paradigm from 'being the face of everything' to 'being a creator of people'. It is only when a critical mass of the organization starts to lead and when teams start becoming accountable that the organization can move towards a breakthrough. And it is only when the leadership is humble that it will allow all others to prosper.

In the simplest, practical terms, humility in the context of leaders is to become irrelevant by creating leaders.

A self-possessed leader who lacks humility may be able to perform too, but only up to a certain level and at a certain scale. Beyond this stage, more often than not, there is a need for further leadership to emerge at the lower levels of the organization. The leader just does not have the requisite trust to inspire leadership, nor does she have the character. The reason is her paradigm of leadership: it has no place for humility.The leader wants to be the 'face' of everything. Then so be it. But this person is not your breakthrough leader. This person is not a leader. She is just a title-holder.

Many argue that Steve Jobs was like this. It is said that he was the face of everything and he succeeded. This is an absolutely misplaced notion. If you speak to the people in Apple, you will hear that Steve Jobs made them constantly achieve more than they thought they would. He did so not by micro-managing, but by making people believe and lead. In my opinion, he did micro-manage quality, but not people.

Do what you say and say what you did; do the right thing rather than the acceptable one; and have enough humility to allow others to lead—in the absence of these principles, a leader cannot inspire trust.

(b) The second imperative for building a successful culture is to unleash talent and build team accountability.

The question of unleashing talent and building team accountability has been discussed under the third reason for the failure of organizations. A culture based on individual accountability blocks the value that an organization can derive from synergy.

How does a leader build teams and unleash potential? This issue has three aspects.

One aspect that has already been discussed is that the leader must be prepared to be irrelevant, at least operationally, and allow other leaders to emerge. This involves a change in the leader's mindset. Unless her mindset changes, the leader will not be able to unleash talent or build complementary teams.

This brings us to our second point: a leader must build complementary teams. A complementary team is one in which the leader's strengths are productive and her weaknesses are made irrelevant through others.

Far too often, we see leadership teams wanting people down the line to 'fall in line' with the leaders' thought process. This essentially implies that generally, a person whose ideas are radically different or who challenges certain decisions or policies is considered an outcast.

This is not the right way of going about things. The problem that most organizations face and the reason why they stagnate is that everyone thinks alike and becomes a prisoner of the organizational culture. This is an outcome of following a formal authority map.

A leader needs to create teams that are complementary. Synergy between teams is possible only if they are complementary, with each one possessing its unique strength. If all of them have similar thoughts, processes, values, ideas and ideologies—or have been forced to have them—then logically, they have less of a need to function synergistically because each team individually will feel that it can do a better job of solving the problem.

What is needed is to create a team in which people have complementary strengths and then create cross functional teams that are complementary and then make them accountable as a whole.

That brings us to the third aspect, which is that a leader must make teams accountable. This is a monumental paradigm shift.

We are used to creating and operating in cultures in which we hold individuals accountable. However, the success of your organization actually depends on whether your teams succeed vertically and then horizontally. If the teams do not succeed as a whole, the success of the organization depends on a few individuals, and this is not a sustainable situation.

It is not sustainable because over a period of time, these individuals will either simply lose their motivation, spark or ability to find answers to new problems, or will burn out or leave.

The answer lies in making teams as a whole accountable to the organization and to each other. If a team is accountable and assessed for its overall output, then the team members automatically hold each other accountable. A leader needs to create a complementary team, in which people collectively look for better solutions, in which they are free to interact and communicate, and in which they are not thinking of what the 'boss' wants to hear, that is, they are thinking of the right thing to do rather than the acceptable thing to do. Only then can a team be capable of achieving a breakthrough.

Following the core principle of moral leadership, that is creating leaders together with making the teams accountable, will have two positive results. First, it will unleash talent and second, it will build synergy. Both are essential composites of sustainable success.

The whole must be greater than the sum of the parts. That is synergy.

In the last couple of years during my research for this book, I have been directly involved in creating such teams. In my experience, in the absence of an individual goal, or rather, in the presence of a team goal—which is now everyone's singular focus and criterion for achievement—there were five things that happened, provided the leader was assuming moral leadership.

(i) The team's goal or output took center stage.

(ii) The end result or the delivery of the end result became the hero for everyone.

(iii) People felt empowered in the true sense. They felt free to contribute to any and every task. There was no 'my' task.

(iv) The teams and people were far more creative and innovative while looking for solutions because the problem was now everyone's problem.

(v) These teams always achieved the goal.

How do you handle the non-performing people in such teams? You do not. The teams do.

(c) The third imperative for building a successful culture is to build an emotional connect.

It is a leader's responsibility to remain true to an organization's purpose, values and vision, and to get the people to connect to these emotionally. If the people do not emotionally relate to the goals, then something needs to be changed—either the organization's leadership or its purpose.

The root causes of an organization's failure to build an

emotional connect with its people are described below.

(i) Unclear purpose, unarticulated roles

To be able to engage people and get them excited, an organization needs to have a purpose and mission that is inspiring in the first place. It needs to have a vision that people want to be a part of. It then needs to remain true to its core values and encourage achievement without violating the basic human values. It also needs to stretch its goals and encourage achievement, which would reinforce its purpose and vision.

Coming up with all this is the easy part. Most organizations would be capable of it, and if not, there are simple ways out. This in itself, however, is not enough to make people feel emotionally connected to the organization and its mission.

People need to believe that the organization is moving towards its vision and for this, the and organization needs a road map.

In the absence of a road map and direction, no one will feel emotionally connected. People believe something when they see it, not when they hear you talk about it. People believe in something when they are engaged in it, and not when they are merely told about it.

Most organizations start out with fancy goals and visions, and then almost instantly, shift their focus to their current preoccupations. It is almost as if they tend to channelize the energy created by their dreams into fulfilling an agenda. By doing this, they lose the people's emotional involvement forever.

As mentioned earlier, what is needed is a road map, a strategic blueprint that can be followed to realize the vision. In the absence of this, everything else that you do to realize your vision is just lip service. Let alone the people, I doubt that even the leader would believe in a vision without a plan.

To achieve an emotional connect, to really get people to believe in the organization's vision and to make them feel excited about being a part of something great, an organization needs to:

| Develop a great vision of what they will achieve

| Break this down into goals for every team in the organization, i.e. chalk out how they will contribute to this vision

| Draw up a strategic actionable map of how this vision will be achieved—for the organization and for each of the teams.

There are two things to be kept in mind. First, people are not interested in how the shareholders' wealth should be maximized. They want to know how the organization will make a difference.

Second, as a leader, you should be able to articulate each department's and each person's role in achieving the vision. If you cannot, it means one of two things—either you do not know and have not yet thought about it, or a particular person in some department does not have a role to play. Either way you will lose the emotional connect.

To sum up, the first step towards building an emotional connect is to create a purpose—one that is compelling enough. Next, the leader must draw up a strategic map that makes people believe that the purpose is achievable.

(ii) Lack of alignment of goals

When we are trying to create a culture of synergy through complementary teams, it is almost a given that this is based on goals which are aligned. This may seem obvious to a leader, who may feel that the goals have already been aligned.

However, if you go to any organization or any of its departments and speak to anyone there, you will discover that the person is unaware of how his goals relate to those of other departments, and how the goals of all the departments relate to those of the organization. If she does not understand these links, then she is neither emotionally connected to the organization's goals, nor aligned to the goals in any way.

Why is it important for people to be aligned to the goals? Everyone needs to share the organization's vision to be able to connect to it emotionally. To allow this to happen, the leader must align the goals as this will help create synergy between the people, which, in turn, will help accomplish the organization's mission. If the goals are not aligned, there will be no such synergy, and the people will then fall into the rut of following the old map of individual accountability.

The moment a leader adopts a culture marked by overcritical and frenetic reviews of performance, talking only about what went wrong, she kills the emotional connect.

To make people connect emotionally with the organization and with each other, the leader must not only align the goals, but must also ensure that everyone understands how the goals are aligned and how to contribute to the organization's purpose and vision. Only then can an organization inculcate a sense of belonging, promote teamwork and create synergy.

(iii) Talking more about failures than about successes.

Far too often, the leadership is overcritical of the organization's performance, achievements and efforts. To criticize has become a norm in review meetings. I think leaders take pride in pulling down the person being reviewed and pointing out her flaws. They probably feel that that is their job.

This is a byproduct of leadership by authority. It's sick. It's sick because it is not even remotely connected to providing leadership; it is a pure display of authority.

Leadership should be a service you provide to a follower through which she can rise above what she believes she is capable of.

The moment a leader adopts a culture marked by overcritical and frenetic reviews of performance, talking only about what went wrong, she kills the emotional connect. This is only natural—if people do not feel good about meeting their leaders, how can they possibly connect to the vision he talks about.

Success breeds success. People will be successful when they feel successful.

Of course, a leader should talk about what went wrong and

promptly take corrective action. However, she must consider this question: when people meet her, do they walk out feeling successful or feeling lousy? Which feeling would you rather have your organization be associated with?

It is far more important to celebrate what people have achieved than to criticize them for what they could not do. In fact, I believe that it is important to celebrate good failures rather than condemn them.

A leader must make people and teams feel that they are successful. It is true that continuous feedback is a must, as is corrective action, but the leader should be aware that by and large, if the people in the organization feel that they are not doing well, then they will not do well. Period.

(iv) Leadership by authority, and not morals

This has been discussed earlier and I will just summarize it for your reference.

A culture of leadership by authority is not conducive to the development of an emotional connection with the organization and its vision. At best, it will encourage people to pretend to feel such a connection out of fear.

Only a moral leader, who focuses on creating more leaders out of genuine feeling and respect for human potential, will be able to build a real emotional connect among the people.

Leaders who lead by authority are not true leaders. It is only a matter of time before both the people and the organization realize this. Such leaders are title-holders. They earn a lot—a lot of disrespect.

People will be successful when they feel successful.

Summary: The three imperatives for building a successful culture through moral leadership are to inspire trust, unleash talent and build team accountability, and build an emotional connect.

When I speak about these findings or present them to people, I am often asked the following questions.

How do we change things?

What needs to be changed?

How do we change from a map of individual accountability to one of synergy?

How do we become a value-driven organization?

How do we adopt a correct map of leadership?

How do we undo what has already been done?

In my experience, the journey of changing an organization's culture begins right at the top. In fact, the first mistake that needs to be corrected is our definition of the role of the CEO (by CEO, I mean the person at the helm, whether you call her the CEO or the Managing Director). .This is the fifth reason for an organization's failure to achieve its goals.

5

The role of the CEO is ill defined

The CEO has no role

The CEO has no role, and as I have stated earlier, the leader's job should be to make herself irrelevant. CEOs attach far too much importance to themselves and their role. The closer the leader of the pack moves towards minimizing her role, the greater will be the degree of effectiveness with which he will be able to dispense his duties.

It is precisely due to the fact that the CEO has no role that she holds the most critical position in an organization. CEOs feel extremely tempted to assume a role. Those who appoint the CEO have a strong tendency to assign her an objective. The peer group of the chief derives immense comfort from letting her make as many decisions as possible.

Due to these three factors—i.e. the CEO's urge to assume a role, the support he receives for this by being assigned an objective, and the further encouragement she receives by being given the power to make innumerable decisions—the CEO misses out on a monumental insight: "I don't have a role."

Let us see how this happens. Allow me to take you through three very recent cases that I have observed quite carefully.

I was providing consultancy services to a large manufacturing company. This organization had ambitious plans, invested heavily in expanding capacity to achieve its goals, hired the best of talent and had somewhat reached the initial targets too. In spite of the fact that the company had reached its targets, it found that its market share had declined, which basically meant that everyone in the industry was growing and there was nothing special about this particular organization.

In the face of the declining market share, significant pressure on profit margins and an alarming rate of attrition, it was decided that it was time to look for a new CEO. A CEO with a solid background in sales was hired. He asked, "What is my role? What do you expect?" The response of the interview board, headed by the vice chairman, was prompt: "Increase the market share, restore profits and do it quick time." The entire hierarchy of the organization was being questioned and condemned day in and day out for the declining market share, but everyone was now happy to allow their new boss to do all the deciding. This became an example of 'leading by authority'.

The CEO was determined. He had an impeccable record and this challenge would be no different. Frequent meetings. Meticulous analysis. Incessant reviews. New sales force. Attractive distributor schemes. Anything and everything that could be done to increase sales was done.

Two years since then, the sales have increased. The market share is down by one per cent more. Attrition is at 31%. The CEO's role is clearly defined, clearer than ever—fix the mess, increase the market share and restore profits.

Two years ago, I was hired by the newly appointed director of an academic institution to resolve conflicts amongst the faculty members. The earlier director had allegedly run the institution in a misguided manner and encouraged a culture that was highly self-centered, leading to infighting among the faculty members and the formation of power centers among the students. As a result, the faculty, which was very capable, was upset and insecure. The reputation of the institute was beginning to suffer. Financial irregularities were quite rampant.

The trustees finally appointed a new director. Having been misguided by the previous administration, they formed a governing council to keep a close watch over the new administration.

During the various meetings that I had with the director and subsequently, the head of human resources, I felt that we were quite in agreement that what was needed was a sense of purpose, the restoration of the value system and a clearly defined path forward.

Interestingly, the council did define the path forward. Unfortunately, it consisted of corporate minds which were interested in the comparison between 'not-for-profit' and 'for-profit' organizations. The path forward was clear: sort out the mess so that we can increase the number of students and run at full capacity. They spoke of developing an alternative stream of revenue from corporate education. The role was thus assigned. The role was also accepted. The decisions followed. The strengths of the academic institution did not match these objectives.

A year later, the state of the institution had improved. However, this had not been the objective. Eventually, everyone got fed up. The governing council was trying to adopt the academician's mindset of trying to make the institution a better place for students, while the academicians were influenced by the governing council's insistence on financial models. Frustrated by constantly trying to patch up the two sides and failing as far as the council's goals were concerned, the director resigned.

The institute is now waiting for a new director to come and assume the given role, i.e. to set things right, run at full capacity and develop corporate education as an additional stream of revenue.

At one time, I was working with a software company which

had failed to grow for three years. It was almost locked at a certain turnover and could not break the barrier. A year later, it achieved phenomenal results. Let us study what happened in these three years.

Prior to these three years, the company had taken certain decisions related to expansion that had led to huge losses and the erosion of cash reserves. However, it managed to control the situation in time and its next goal was to get back to its former level of cash reserves. It was clear that this goal could be achieved only through growth.

Week after week, month after month and year after year, the management tried to find ways of increasing sales. However, in spite of all the schemes, incentives, marketing and new verticals, the sales remained locked at the same place. It was not that anything wrong was being done. The executives had done the same things in their previous companies and they had led to an increase in sales, but they were just not working here. Why not?

Year after year, the role of the CEO continued to be 'increase sales'. Year after year, the reality remained the same—the company's sales would not increase.

Such situations are not unique. They are commonly faced by most organizations. It is true that practices such as those described above can also bring results, which is why there are misconceptions regarding the path to achievement. However, these results are not necessarily an indication of the right way because the effects of those approaches might take some time to become visible. The economic collapse of the United States is a prime example of this.

If you carefully examine the three cases mentioned above, you will notice that each of these situations was a result of the CEO's failure to fulfill her role. Whether we consider the declining market share of the manufacturing company, the flawed culture at the academic institution or the software company's inability to break past the sales barrier, it is clear that the problem lay in the way that those organizations were managed. The accounting map was at the center of decision-making. What they needed, and what every turnaround needs, is a value-driven map.

When a CEO considers that her foremost responsibility is to increase the market share or sales, her decisions and actions will be aimed primarily at finding solutions to the immediate situation. Most organizations in this reactive mode focus on short-term solutions, such as coming up with schemes or market gimmicks, and giving monetary incentives to employees or dealers. Furthermore, these short-term solutions are strongly associated with shortcuts and contribute to depleting the organization's integrity.

In all the energy that gets directed and redirected through the insane number of meetings and reviews that take place, we end up ignoring one of the most basic questions. (In fact, the first sign of an organization in which the CEO has got mired in a faulty role is the insane number of meetings and reviews that are held.) The question that is ignored is: 'What is the real cause of this situation?" Even if you were to discover a cause, I can guarantee that whatever this cause, the solution does not lie in tricking yourself out of the crisis by resorting to schemes, incentives and bribes.

The problems faced by organizations are itself a result of the CEO not doing what she is supposed to, which, simply put, is to create an organization and culture which deliver a different outcome.

You might be fooled into thinking that the question as to what is the cause of the situation is being asked all the time. Well, in a sense you might be right. The question may be asked. The answer is rarely sought. The reason is simple. The CEO's mandate is to rectify the situation. She would much rather get people to discuss what She thinks will solve the problem than get them to investigate what led to it. After all, what people are patted on the back for at board meetings are initiatives backed by an Excel sheet on returns on investment.

In the three examples mentioned above, the decision was that the CEO be assigned a role to correct the situation. Am I suggesting that this is not needed? Certainly not. Of course the situation needs to be corrected, else there will be no organization left for us to discuss and no CEO whose role we can talk about. However, this need not warrant a definition of the CEO's role.

In fact, they are a result of certain actions of the management, one of which is defining such roles. The problems faced by these organizations are itself a result of the CEO not doing what she is supposed to, which, simply put, is to create an organization and culture which deliver a different outcome.

Everyone has had a certain career path prior to becoming a CEO. All of them must have pursued certain specific areas, such as sales, finance, manufacturing and IT. The natural tendency on being assigned the role of a CEO is to fall back on one's core functional expertise. While there is no harm in using one's knowledge, one must remember that the most successful CEOs have been those who have resisted the temptation to remain in their comfort zone to have operational clarity and have instead, embraced the uncertainties and unknowns.

In the 21st century, an era of management in which the verdicts of Judgment Day are pronounced on the basis of profits and valuations above all else, it is even more imperative for the CEO to be clear about her pursuits. It is this leader, her decisions or absence of decisions, and her actions or inaction that affect the lives of people, the life of the organization and the ecosystem within which the organization operates.

The people in an organization define its mission, values, vision and goals. It is safe to say that an organization, as such, does not have any mission, values, vision and goals. People do. Thus, the degree to which these are pursued at various points in the life cycle of an organization will change depending on how dearly they are cherished by the people. The head of these people is the CEO.

In most cases and in most boards, where the CEO represents the organization, the major topic of discussion is profitability in some form or the other. Yes, profits are very important as making no profits means the end of the company. However, sadly, when profits, market shares or sales numbers become the driving force of the CEO, there is a deterioration in these very parameters. It always will without fail and the reason is very simple.

Profit in pure terms is surplus left in your balance sheet. Profit can be created or increased in two ways. First, an organization receives a certain value for the goods or services it provides. This value can be utilized in a manner that leads to a surplus, i.e. this value or resources acquired through it can be allocated in a profitable manner. Let us call this **allocation** or utilization. Second, more and more incoming value can be created by attracting more customers or increasing the size of the goods or services offered to the existing customers. Let us call this **creation**.

How would a management that is constantly guided predominantly by financial goals, as in the three cases mentioned earlier, look upon allocation and creation? In which areas would it allocate resources? How would it create more customers?

Allocation invariably becomes a matter of conforming to the accounting map and because of the immense pressure to increase numbers, creation becomes a matter of drawing up schemes, resorting to short-term, focused marketing, and conducting business through bribes.

By taking a path that consists of dedicated efforts in the

shape of brainstorming, meetings, reviews, ideation, strategizing for creation through schemes, and incentive plans for employees and dealers, the management's basic assumption is that just because the organization is guided and motivated by profits, others would be driven by a similar greed.

Yes, this model does work for some time. However, it does not provide an organization with any thought leadership. It is not conducive to any innovation to increase value for the customer. It can be replicated by almost anyone, and that is what happens. Thus, it works only in the short term and the gains start to erode thereafter, or at least, it fails to result in growth at the exponential rate that was expected initially.

This clearly explains the failure of the manufacturing company mentioned earlier to increase its market share: the model was so easily replicable that everyone adopted it. It also explains the failure of the academic institution, which overstretched its energies to find ways of filling seats rather than worry about ways of improving the quality of education.

Similarly, it explains the failure of the software company, which was doing nothing wrong and everything was being done on the basis of the employees' past experience in other companies; they just did not know how to deal with a situation in which the market stops responding to schemes. None of the CEOs could manage to make the transition to creating a value-driven organization. They did not bother. It was not on their minds because their mindset was different.

When increasing profits, market shares or sales numbers becomes the role of the CEO, there is bound to be a decline in these very parameters, as mentioned earlier. There will always be such a decline, without fail, and the reason is very simple. The reason is that in attempting to find short-term solutions like these, the real cause of the problem remains undiscovered. Everyone, including the CEO, is so busy doing something that there is no one to just stand back and take an overview. Having invested years of our energy on reactive solutions, we might have strayed a bit too far from the path of pinpointing causes.

The right thing has not entered our minds because our mindset itself is rooted in outdated theory.

Profits are necessary for the existence of an organization. However, profits need to be an outcome of the way an organization is managed rather than the prime reason for which it is managed. Whenever a CEO assumes a particular role either because she has been told to contain a problem or because no one else is available, she is already on the wrong path. She is no longer engaged in building an organization that will deliver the profits. She is now engaged in delivering the profits. This is not sustainable. Organization-building is a special skill. The alternative to it is not trickery.

Let us look at it in a larger perspective. An organization must be profitable to exist. Profits come from the revenue received from customers. Very simply put, an organization must exist to create and serve customers. This is the ultimate objective of any for-profit organization you may come across anywhere in the world. The greater the number of customers, the greater will be the growth and market shares.

What does an organization have that allows it to exist? It has certain resources. These may be capital, people, infrastructure or other assets. What does an organization do to be able to create and serve customers? It can essentially perform three functions: attract resources, utilize resources or transform resources, such that it continually increases value for the customer and thereby, for itself.

The primary role of the CEO of an organization is not to have a role. She has a responsibility and an objective. The objective is (a) to increase value for the customer by attracting resources, for example, attracting people who are best equipped to perform the task at hand (and not necessarily attracting the best talent); (b) to utilize resources (allocate resources to accomplish tasks that need to be achieved); and (c) to transform resources (leverage the performance of all resources).

The objective is to create a value-driven organization by providing moral leadership, that is, by developing or unleashing talent to foster leaders. This can happen only if individual structures are broken down and synergy is created by building accountability in the team. To be able to do this, one has to abandon the tendency to rely solely on an accounting map paradigm.

The CEO's responsibility is to do the right thing, to do things which are in the interest of the organization, and to resist succumbing to role definitions originating from the short-term, greed-inspired definitions of those who have appointed her, because only then will she be able to create an organization that increases value for itself by increasing value for the customers. A CEO who plays this role will create an organization that relies on innovation and the creation of value, which will lead to thought leadership. In no way can such an organization be created by assigning the CEO short-term roles and goals. Such an organization can be created by letting the CEO create it.

The CEO has no role. So what should the role be?

A business cannot exist unless it makes a profit. Period. An organization need not exist to make money, though it must make money to exist in the long term.

As stated earlier, the role of an organization is to attract, utilize and transform resources such that it can create greater value for its customers and for itself. The role of the CEO is to create an organization that keeps doing this. Her role is not to do this herself, but to create an organization which does this.

Why is this necessary? Almost all organizations, know that they need to be profitable. Profits come from growth. The organization's leaders are assigned the role of achieving 'growth'. The 'quarter-on-quarter' assessment pushes the CEO to start thinking along the lines of achieving growth and delivering accordingly. This, in turn, forces the entire system to embrace short-term measures, whether knowingly or unknowingly.

Thus, people start thinking in this manner because they want growth and want it before the next quarterly review. The question they fail to consider is obvious—what will really make the organization grow? What will make the organization grow consistently is not tactics, schemes and a few quick wins, but the creation of value.

Everyone in the industry reaches a similar 'value level' sooner or later. Thus, no organization is left with much of an advantage in terms of a competitive edge or leverage for its product or service. This naturally means that the only way to increase profitability now is through better cost management. As a result, the CEO's role is defined as increasing 'profitability'.

The quarter-on-quarter reviews will ensure that short-term action is taken with respect to fixed costs, purchases, raw material sourcing, etc. The strategy might show results, too. The organization may even pat itself on the back for its strategic master stroke. How much more naive can it get? This is exactly what happens in most companies that stagnate or disappear.

The role of the CEO is to become irrelevant.

Organization stagnates because it is no longer able to acquire customers at a greater pace. An organization will grow either if it draws more customers or is able to get more from its existing customers. In either case, growth will occur when the customers get greater value.

An organization exists because its customers do.

Customers exist because they get value.

An organization can grow consistently if value does.

Value is multidimensional and does not refer to just a single aspect (for example, product or quality). As stated earlier, every department must be value-driven or less inconspicuous.

The leader of an organization has to be the custodian of this value. He also has to be the custodian of the leverage the organization will derive from the value. The leader of the organization thus has to attract, utilize and transfer the resources available to deliver greater value and gain greater leverage.

The role of the CEO is to create an organization that keeps doing this. Her job is to create an organization that does this, instead of doing it herself. In other words, the role of the CEO is to become irrelevant. The CEO has to provide moral leadership and create more leaders, and the leaders have to ensure that it is the teams that are accountable and not individuals.

When the board reviews the CEO's performance, instead of asking, "Why are the numbers down?" wouldn't it be far better to ask, "What was done this quarter to increase customer value? How is the company performing in the marketplace?"

And instead of asking, "Who are the star performers?" wouldn't it be far better to ask, "Who are the best performing teams and how can their success be replicated in other teams?"

6

Entrepreneurial thinking – the universal misnomer

In our interviews during the research for this book with the business leaders, developing entrepreneurial thinking emerged as a very popular solution to their problems of lack of desired achievement. Therefore I thought it appropriate to include the topic in this book as I felt that very few leaders really understand entrepreneurial thinking.

"Lets create Entrepreneurial thinking in our organization."

This is a very popular buzz-word in modern day board rooms.

The intent of entrepreneurism is wonderful. As was revealed to us, it is inspired by businesses and teams promising to but not reaching their stated goals.

The assumption that managements make is that entrepreneurial mindset may well be the answer.

But do they understand entrepreneurial thinking?

Do they know what it means?
If people had that mindset, wouldn't they be entrepreneurs?

Do they know how to develop this thinking?

Is asking Human Resources to do some programs going to be enough?

Where should they begin?

I can almost guarantee that none of the people who perpetuate the need for entrepreneurial thinking can explain entrepreneurial thinking in one paragraph or in one thousand paragraphs. They can't.

No one has really understood it.

Having said that, is entrepreneurial thinking important? Lets examine it here.

Its puzzling to me that when I meet, interview, train and coach business leaders across industries that almost all of them eat, sleep and breathe business goals and targets, yet almost none of them achieve the original goal that they had set for the year.

The reasons might be many and as explained in the previous chapters, their business outcomes tend to define the role of a CEO and this takes her further and further away from creating an organization that build value for itself by building value for its customers.

The CEO then mostly falls into the trap of doing the acceptable thing.

An answer to creating a an organization that has sustained business growth probably does lie in some measure to creating entrepreneurial thinking in the organization as a whole. The leaders of course must take the lead.

Lets examine a situation where a leader has been asked to achieve certain targets for the quarter on priority. Lets assume that she falls short a few quarters in a row. What happens next?

The reviewers get angry and lose their patience. What does the leader do? The leader naturally has reasons why the targets haven't been met. These reasons typically begin with organization's internal issues and previous cultures. Over a period of time these reasons shift to being external because the reviewing board considers the internal reasons to be within the domain of the leader.

Facing the heat over numbers, the leader loses sight of internal corrections and isn't able to completely focus on doing the right things. By now the pressure is mounting. So where do these reasons shift? They shift outside.

The CEO or the management begins to point out reasons such as a bad economy, non availability of talent or outdated technology or processes which typically require huge amount of capital investments to rectify.

Over a period of little time the rest of the people begin to echo these reasons as well, they start to believe them too.

I am not suggesting that these reasons might not be real. They well might be, but, there is a problem in this new found belief. The problem is that the management has lost sight of the root cause. Now, even if they were to correct these reasons, the root cause still remains and hence no substantial business gains will be visible post correction.

What is this root cause?

The root causes mostly lie in following an incorrect map or in not being a value-driven company or in having a highly individualistic culture or in authoritative leadership.

The board slams, "Create entrepreneurial thinking."

What they really mean by this statement is, "Find a way."

What they probably assume is that a person who thinks or acts like an entrepreneur will probably not accept failure and would find some way or the other to turn the situation around.

For an entrepreneur, failure is not an option.

A successful entrepreneur probably will. This is a reason enough to emulate their thinking.

Though the assumption on entrepreneurial thinking that is made by almost everyone is far from the truth.

Examine this - An entrepreneur usually fails in more things than those that he succeeds in.

Are organizations going to allow this entrepreneurial thinking?

An entrepreneur takes risks, experiments and these usually result in cash burn.

Are organizations going to allow this entrepreneurial thinking?

An entrepreneur makes decisions that might significantly back fire?

Are organizations going to allow this entrepreneurial thinking?

An entrepreneur in a majority of situations is driven by 'gut feel' more than he or she is driven by 'analytics'.

Are organizations going to allow this entrepreneurial thinking?

A successful entrepreneur learns though these experiences to be eventually successful.

Yes, the fact is that an entrepreneurial mindset is trained to find a way. That training is fundamentally rooted in entrepreneurial experience. That experience is flooded with setbacks. Will organizations allow those setbacks?

On one hand, each and every failure is criticized in the boardroom. On the other hand you want the same people to be entrepreneurs.

On one hand the CEO herself and her management team reprimands failures. On the other hand they expect to create people who will 'find a way'.

It doesn't work like that.

Imagine if Edison was answerable to a reprimanding manager, if he was managed by a leader who condemned failure. If that had happened then Edison might not have invented the light bulb for he failed 10000 times to create it.

Imagine if Henry Ford reported to a 'failure despising' board. If that had happened then Ford would have needed as many bailout packages as GM.

Does entrepreneurial thinking work?

Of course it does. Essentially entrepreneurial thinking, mindset and belief is this - **That failure is not an option**.

Failure is not an option for a successful entrepreneur. Its through that mechanism that they become successful. Yes they have setbacks. Yes they fail too as I wrote earlier, some many times over, but they eventually find a way because failure isn't an option.

This is vastly different from those who are in executive jobs. Failure is an option here. In fact in most cases, there is no sense of failure. People blame it on some issue or the other, move on to the next job, as an executive, perhaps at a better designation and salary. What failure?

The entrepreneur will stick it out, innovate, improvise, create and find a way. Eventually.

The Board, the CEO and the management might be hoping to create that spirit of entrepreneurs. Though if you are to create entrepreneurial thinking in an organization, then

you will have to create a culture that embraces failures, where people are free to make mistakes,

you will have to create an organization that gives people the freedom to experiment,

you will have to break down the control hierarchies that exist in the structure which curtail this freedom,

you will have to instill a sense of passion in people that failure is not an option - yes there are setbacks and that is acceptable,

you will have to enable and empower people when they fail, not by reprimanding them but by finding them solutions to turn it around,

you will have to create an organization that does the right things, not just the acceptable things

In our research for this book, we had interviewed over seventy business leaders. We had asked all of them on their opinion about entrepreneurial thinking. All of them agreed that its needed and will be a great bonus. Almost all of them in some words or the other described entrepreneurial thinking as 'finding a way'. None of them could articulate how to create it.

The reason for this is that they are expecting a result (namely entrepreneurial thinking) without dealing with the real causes that block free spirit. These real causes are the ones outlined earlier in the book under why organizations fail.

People will learn to think differently when they are allowed to operate with freedom, that is when they are not afraid to fail.

Its common sense to allow entrepreneurial spirit to foster in an organization. Its common nonsense that the very people who scream about entrepreneurial thinking are the ones who kill it.

Entrepreneurial thinking or an attitude of 'finding a way' or a mindset that 'failure is not an option' or behaviors of 'innovation and creativity' are absolutely essential and almost non negotiable for an organization that aims to outperform the industry and the economy.

Its common sense to allow entrepreneurial spirit to foster in an organization.

Its common nonsense that the very people who scream about entrepreneurial thinking are the ones who kill it.

However, it is our conclusion that entrepreneurial thinking, innovation and creativity are not the root causes of *Why organizations fail to reach their stated goals.* These are end results or by products of doing the right things or of creating the right culture as outlined in the first five chapters.

Entrepreneurial thinking, attitude, mindset and behavior requires transformation of human beings and the culture they create. At the helm of this culture are the leaders.

It has to be the most critical aspects of the role of leadership to create this culture. A delegation of duties by any CEO on the subject of transforming human beings or of transforming the organization in this manner would be an abdication of the role itself.

7

Compromise is not a solution

A lot of leaders and companies come to consult me and many appreciate my point. They feel determined to make changes and even get quick results. Yet in their effort to make things happen quickly, they compromise.

It is important for leaders to know that compromises will not get them anywhere and there are no shortcuts. The path is simple—create superior value, create moral leadership and create a successful culture, and then gain leverage.

The shortcuts people take include rushing through the analysis of what might be the value of the company's products/services to the customer. Quick judgments are made and nobody takes the pains to visit the markets and customers. This is a form of compromise.

The shortcuts people take include directing internal change without understanding and analyzing the internal realities. Internal change entails a cultural change. People are skeptical of the CEO. Leaders often tend to delegate the responsibility for bringing about this change to the human resources personnel, relying wholesale on their programs and not without realizing that the CEO is the chief officer of the people. It is the CEO who needs to lead the change. Her not doing so is a form of compromise.

People often take shortcuts because of their inability to stand their ground with the board. Together, the CEO and the board make some 'patch-up' deal. In response to the CEO's idea, the board says, "Yes, do that, but in the meantime, till your actions produce results, for this year, let the focus be solely on the short-term objectives." This is a compromise—the end of the story.

Compromise is not a solution. There can be no midway role for the leader or the organization. There is no midway value for the customer. There are no midway results for the business. There is nothing such as a half-right solution.

In implementing any of the solutions suggested in this book, one must take care not to compromise. The solution works as a whole and not as a part.

I remember that not so long ago, the largest business in India was divided between two brothers after their father passed away. After months of protracted negotiations, a deal was struck. The headlines in the morning newspaper read, "Compromise reached. Solution found." That was far from the truth. It was a compromise. It was a division of business. There was no solution.

Divide by two is not an answer.

Compromise is not a solution. It is a compromise.

About The Author

Chetan is recognized by the corporate world as an educator, a consultant. He is a foremost authority on strategic business growth.

He has partnered with many International small and large companies. His principles and methodologies have been applied in almost every area of human endeavor from industry to education to the social sector. And while Chetan is indeed a success partner, he is first and foremost aphilosopher. He is a thinker who provokes others to do the same.

You can contact the author at Chetan@fq.biz

www.ingramcontent.com/pod-product-compliance
Lightning Source LLC
Chambersburg PA
CBHW021438170526
45164CB00001B/293